MW00449413

Evidence-Based Inquiry Using Primary Sources

Grade 2

Credits
Author: Jeanette Moore Ritch, MS Ed.
Copy Editor: Sandra Ogle

Visit *carsondellosa.com* for correlations to Common Core, state, national, and Canadian provincial standards.

Carson-Dellosa Publishing, LLC
PO Box 35665
Greensboro, NC 27425 USA
carsondellosa.com

ISBN 978-1-4838-2397-3
01-106157784

Table of Contents

Introduction

The primary sources shown in this book represent glimpses of real life. They are photos of actual people, posters that once hung on storefronts, paintings that interpret history, and ads or articles taken from newspapers in circulation in another era. All primary sources shown here are from the archives of the Library of Congress.

This book includes 15 primary sources. Each is accompanied by the same story written at three levels (below grade level, on grade level, and above grade level) for differentiation. Distribute the versions according to students' abilities. The final page of each selection offers prompts and questions about the primary source and/or text and can be used for all levels with some assistance.

This book is full of opportunities for inquiry-based learning. Inquiry-based learning is a process of active learning that greatly improves reading comprehension skills. Allow the primary sources reproduced on these pages to speak for themselves. Then, allow the natural curiosity of students to do the rest.

The role of the teacher in inquiry-based learning is that of facilitator. Teachers are encouraged to first present the primary source without much accompanying information. Encourage students to ask questions, look for answers, and make connections between the past and the present. Prompt students to think critically about what they are viewing. Let them make inferences from the details, share varying points of view, draw conclusions, and connect known facts with details in the visuals shown.

Performance Rubric

Use this rubric as a guide for assessing students' engagement with each primary source unit.

4	_____ Notes details and evaluates primary source critically
	_____ Displays avid curiosity about photo and topic
	_____ Makes or disproves connections between primary source and personal experiences or prior knowledge
	_____ Exhibits high-level thinking skills when responding to *Investigate, Question,* and *Understand* prompts
3	_____ Notes details and evaluates primary source superficially
	_____ Displays average curiosity about photo and topic
	_____ Makes mostly obvious connections between primary source and personal experiences or prior knowledge
	_____ Responds with adequate insight to *Investigate, Question,* and *Understand* prompts
2	_____ Notes some details but does not evaluate primary source
	_____ Displays some curiosity about photo and topic
	_____ Makes few connections between primary source and personal experiences or prior knowledge
	_____ Responds without insight or high-level thinking to *Investigate, Question,* and *Understand* prompts
1	_____ Notes few details and does not evaluate primary source
	_____ Displays no curiosity about photo and topic
	_____ Makes no connections between primary source and personal experiences or prior knowledge
	_____ Shows little interest in or is unable to respond thoughtfully to *Investigate, Question,* and *Understand* prompts

How to Use This Book

Teachers may wish to prompt students to study each primary source before reading the accompanying text. Students can write or ask questions as they study the documents or photographs. Spark their curiosity with discussion about the elements of the primary source. Students may then discover more information in the text. An inquiry page follows each set of texts and provides three levels of prompts: *Investigate, Question,* and *Understand.* Allow time and opportunity for students to answer their own questions and to find out more in books, magazines, and on safe Internet sources.

Let's Go to the Library

Libraries have been in America for a long time! A library has a lot of books. People read there. Boys and girls can take books home. Then, they have to bring the books back.

Libraries did not always have computers. There were places to sit and read. There was art. There were rooms for meetings. There were newspapers.

This photograph of a library was taken in 1910. It is in Manhattan. That is in New York City. There are boys and girls. They are in a building on Henry Street. The boys and girls read books together. They do their work. They are students.

© Carson-Dellosa • CD-104860 • Evidence-Based Inquiry Using Primary Sources

Let's Go to the Library

Libraries have been in America for hundreds of years. A library has many books. People read there. Boys and girls can take books home. Then, they have to bring the books back.

Libraries then did not have computers. There were places to sit and read. There was art hanging on the walls. There were rooms for people to hold meetings. There were newspapers.

This is a photograph of a library taken in 1910. It was in Manhattan. It is in New York City. There are boys and girls. They are in a building on Henry Street. The boys and girls read books together at the tables. They do their work. They are students.

Library of Congress, LC-USZ62-48787

Let's Go to the Library

Libraries have been in America for close to 300 years! A library is a place full of books. People can read there or take books home. Boys and girls can use the books for a few days. Then, the books have to go back.

Libraries long ago did not have computers. There were places to sit and read. The children in the picture are reading and writing. The library is a good place to do this.

This photo was taken in 1910. It was in Manhattan. It is in New York City. The children are in a building on Henry Street. They are in the library. They read books together.

Name _____

Let's Go to the Library

 Investigate

1. What do you see in this photo?

    _____

    _____

2. What did you see first? Why?

    _____

    _____

? **Question**

3. Look at the photo. What do you want to learn more about?

    _____

    _____

4. Do you go to the library? How do you decide when to go?

    _____

    _____

 Understand

5. What do you think the children are doing at the library?

    _____

    _____

6. Look at the library and books, the children, and the teacher. What do you see that is different from today's libraries and people?

    _____

    _____

Traffic Police

Traffic police work in busy towns. They are in cities. They help people stay safe on the roads. They watch cars. They watch trucks. They ask drivers to slow down.

Long ago, traffic police helped people too. This was before there were lots of cars. The streets had wagons with horses. There were people on bikes. Lots of people walked too.

This photo is from 1911. There is a man. He is a traffic policeman. He is on a street in New York City. He holds his left hand up. That means "stop"! The man in the horse-drawn wagon stops. The policeman wants to let three girls cross the street. The girls are safe.

Traffic Police

Traffic police work in busy towns and cities. They help people stay safe on the roads. They watch cars and trucks. They tell drivers to slow down.

Long ago, traffic police helped people before there were lots of cars. The streets had wagons with horses and bicycles. Lots of people walked too.

This photo is from 1911. There is a man. He is a traffic policeman. He is on a street in New York City. He holds his left hand up. That means "stop"! The man in the horse-drawn wagon stops. The policeman wants to let three girls cross the street. The girls are safe.

Library of Congress, LC-USZ62-123183

Traffic Police

Traffic police work in busy towns and cities. They help people stay safe on the roads. They watch cars and trucks. They tell drivers to slow down.

Long ago, traffic police helped people before there were lots of cars. The streets had wagons with horses and bicycles. Lots of people walked too.

This photo was taken in 1911. There is a policeman. The policeman is in New York City. He holds his hand up. That means "stop"! The man in the horse-drawn wagon stops. The policeman also has his other hand up. He wants to let three girls cross the street. The girls are safe.

● ● ●

Traffic Police

 Investigate

1. What do you see in this photo?

   _____

   _____

2. What did you see first? Why?

   _____

   _____

? Question

3. Look at the picture. What do you want to learn more about?

   _____

   _____

4. What do traffic police do?

   _____

   _____

 Understand

5. Why is the policeman holding up his left and right hands?

   _____

   _____

6. How does this street corner look different from a street corner you have seen?

   _____

   _____

Class Time

Most kids learned at home hundreds of years ago. Some kids had tutors. Some kids had teachers come to their homes. Some kids were taught by parents. By the 1800s, kids went to school. Not everyone went to school. Some kids worked on farms. Some worked in factories.

In 1918, many kids had to go to elementary school. They learned to read. They learned to write. They learned math. Most teachers were women.

This photo is from 1899. It was taken at a school in Washington, DC. Girls and boys are in the class. Everyone is dressed up! The teacher is a woman. She has a dog. The kids look at the dog. Do you have a dog in your class?

Library of Congress, LC-USZ62-39163

Class Time

Most kids learned at home hundreds of years ago. Some children had tutors. Some children had teachers come to their homes. Some children were taught by their parents. Then, in the 1800s, boys and girls went to school. Not everyone went to school. Some children worked on farms. Some boys and girls worked in factories.

By 1918, many children had to go to elementary school. They learned to read. They learned to write. They learned math. Most teachers were women.

This photo is from 1899. It was taken at a school in Washington, DC. Girls and boys are in the class. Everyone is dressed up! The teacher is a woman. She has a dog. Do you have a dog in your class?

Library of Congress, LC-USZ62-39163

Class Time

Most kids learned at home hundreds of years ago. Some children had tutors. Some children had teachers come to their homes, and other children were taught by their parents. Then, in the 1800s, boys and girls went to school. But, not everyone went to school. Some children worked on family farms. Some boys and girls even worked in factories.

By 1918, many children had to go to an elementary school. They learned to read. They learned to write. They learned skills for solving math problems. Most teachers were women.

This photo is from 1899. It was taken at a school in Washington, DC. Girls and boys are in the class. Everyone is dressed up! The teacher is a woman. She has a dog in the front of the classroom. Do you have a dog in your class?

● ● ●

Class Time

 Investigate

1. What do you see in this photo?

   _____

   _____

2. What did you see first? Why?

   _____

   _____

 Question

3. Look at the photo. What do you want to learn more about?

   _____

   _____

4. Why do you think a dog is in the classroom?

   _____

   _____

 Understand

5. What do you think the kids are learning about?

   _____

   _____

6. How is your classroom like this classroom? How is it different?

   _____

   _____

Kids at Work

Today, kids go to school. Many children 100 years ago went to school. But, many did not. They had to go to work like grown-ups!

By 1890, many children had to work. They worked in factories. They worked in stores. They worked on farms. They worked on boats. They had to work for as many as 14 hours in one day! This was not good for children at all.

This photo is from 1911. It is in a town called Dunbar. It is in Louisiana. The girl on the left is Rosy. She is eight years old. She is shucking oysters. That means she is opening them with a knife. That is not safe! She is with other children. Do you see the baby?

Library of Congress, LC-USZ62-12875

Kids at Work

Today, kids go to school. Many children 100 years ago went to school. But, many did not. They had to go to work like grown-ups!

By 1890, many children had to work. They worked in factories. They worked in stores. They worked on farms. They worked on boats. They had to work for as many as 14 hours in one day! This was not good for children at all.

This photo is from 1911. It is in Dunbar, Louisiana. The girl on the left is Rosy. She is eight years old. She has to work many hours each day. She is shucking oysters. That means she is opening them with a knife. It is very dangerous. She is with many other children. There is even a baby!

Library of Congress, LC-USZ62-12875

Kids at Work

Today, children go to school. Many children 100 years ago went to school too. But, many did not. They had to go to work like grown-ups!

By 1890, many children had to work. They worked in factories. They worked in stores. They worked on farms. They worked on boats. They had to work for many hours, from the morning until the evening.

This photo is from 1911. It is in Dunbar, Louisiana. The girl on the left is Rosy. She is eight years old. She has to work many hours each day. She is shucking oysters. That means she is opening them with a knife. It is very dangerous. She is with many other children. There is even a baby!

Library of Congress, LC-USZ62-12875

Name _____

Kids at Work

 Investigate

1. What do you see in this photo?

   _____

   _____

2. What did you see first? Why?

   _____

   _____

 **Question**

3. Look at the photo. What do you want to learn more about?

   _____

   _____

4. Why do you think the kids are working?

   _____

   _____

 Understand

5. What are the kids wearing?

   _____

   _____

6. What kinds of people are in the picture?

   _____

   _____

Animal Food

Do you know what farm animals eat? Each animal enjoys healthy food. Sometimes their food is called "feed." It keeps the animals strong.

Cattle, or cows, like to eat grass and hay. Grass and hay have lots of fiber. Cows eat grains and corn. They like oats. Horses like oats too. They like to eat grass like cows. They also eat grain.

This print was made in the 1880s. It was printed in color. The sign has writing on it. It is a sign for animal food. It is an ad for farmers to read. It tells them to buy the food. The sign has a black horse. There are also chickens. The animals are hungry. They want Gordon's animal food!

Animal Food

Do you know what farm animals eat? Each animal enjoys different food. Sometimes their food is called "feed." It keeps the animals healthy.

Cattle, or cows, like to eat grass and hay. There is lots of fiber. Cows eat grains too. They eat barley and corn. They like oats. Horses like oats too. They do like to eat grass. They also like to eat hay and grain, like cattle.

This print was taken in the 1880s. It was printed in color. It is a sign that advertises food for animals. It is an ad for farmers to read. It tells them to buy the food. The sign has a black horse. There are also chickens. The animals are hungry for Gordon's animal food!

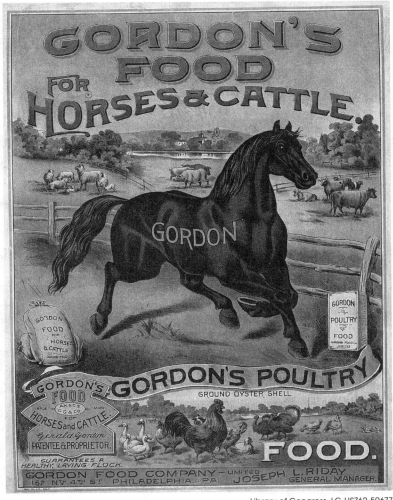

Library of Congress, LC-USZ62-50677

Animal Food

Do you ever wonder what farm animals eat? Each animal enjoys different food. Sometimes their food is called "feed." It keeps the animals strong and healthy.

Cattle, or cows, like to eat roughage. Roughage is grass. It is also hay. A lot of fiber is in their diet. They eat grains too. They eat barley, corn, and oats. Horses are picky eaters. They do like to eat grass. They also like to eat hay and grain, like cattle.

This print was taken in the 1880s. It was printed in color. It is a sign that advertises food for animals. It is an ad for farmers to read. It tells them to buy the food. The sign has a black horse. There are also chickens. The animals are hungry for Gordon's animal food!

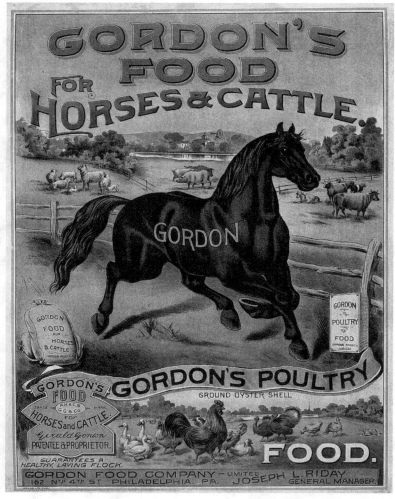

Library of Congress, LC-USZ62-50677

Name _____

Animal Food

 Investigate

1. What do you see in this ad?

   _____

   _____

2. What did you see first? Why?

   _____

   _____

 Question

3. Look at the picture. What do you want to learn more about?

   _____

   _____

4. Did you ever feed a farm animal or pet? When? What did you feed it?

   _____

   _____

Understand

5. Why is "Gordon" printed in the middle of the horse?

   _____

   _____

6. Look at the bottom of the print. What is *poultry*? Are there any other words you do not know? Make a list. Look them up.

   _____

   _____

Gum for Sale!

Kids chewed gum a long time ago. Gum was made from charcoal and chalk! Then, a man named William White made gum better. He added sugar. It made it sweet. He added peppermint.

Later, Tutti-Frutti gum was sold in New York City. Then, a man named William Wrigley sold new gum. It had other flavors. He made Juicy Fruit. He made Wrigley's Spearmint.

This photo is from 1912, more than 100 years ago. There are three boys. They are in Washington, DC. They sell gum. They sell it next to a theater at night. One boy is eight years old. His name is Eli. The other two boys are 10 and 11 years old. Their names are Morris and Harvey. Two of them make 50 cents a night. The boys are workers.

Gum for Sale!

Kids chewed gum a long time ago. Gum was made from charcoal and chalk! Then, a man named William White made gum better. He added sugar. It made it sweet. He added peppermint.

Then, there was Tutti-Frutti gum. It was sold in New York City. Then, a man named William Wrigley sold gum with flavors. He made Juicy Fruit. He made Wrigley's Spearmint.

This photo was taken in 1912, more than 100 years ago. The boys are in Washington, DC. They are selling gum at night. One boy is eight years old. His name is Eli. The other two boys are 10 and 11 years old. Their names are Morris and Harvey. Two of them make 50 cents a night. They sold gum next to a theater.

Library of Congress, LC-DIG-nclc-03752

Gum for Sale!

Kids chewed gum over 100 years ago. First, gum was made from charcoal and chalk! Then, a man named William White made it even better. He added sugar and peppermint.

In the 1880s, there was Tutti-Frutti gum. It was sold in New York City. In the 1890s, William Wrigley made many more flavors. He made Juicy Fruit. He made Wrigley's Spearmint.

This photo was taken in 1912, more than 100 years ago. The boys are in Washington, DC. They are selling gum at night. One boy is eight years old. His name is Eli. The other two boys are 10 and 11 years old. Their names are Morris and Harvey. Two of them make 50 cents a night. They sold gum next to the theater.

Library of Congress, LC-DIG-nclc-03752

Name _____

Gum for Sale!

 Investigate

1. What do you see in this photo?

   _____

   _____

2. What did you see first? Why?

   _____

   _____

 Question

3. Look at the photo. What do you want to learn more about?

   _____

   _____

4. What do you think the boys could buy with 50 cents then?

   _____

   _____

 Understand

5. What are the boys wearing compared to boys in your class? Why?

   _____

   _____

6. Why do you think the boys are working? Why are they working at night?

   _____

   _____

Yellowstone

Yellowstone is a national park. It is so big! It is in three states. It is in Idaho. It is in Montana. It is in Wyoming. The park started in 1872. It was the first national park. The park has geysers. Geysers are springs. Water sprays out of them!

Many animals are in Yellowstone National Park. They live there. There are grizzly bears. There are wolves. There are groups of bison.

This photo is from 1931. There are groups of people. Some are on horses. They look at the canyon. They also look at the Lower Falls of the Yellowstone River. This is in Wyoming.

Library of Congress, LC-USZ62-126295

Yellowstone

Yellowstone is a national park. It is so big! It is in three states. It is in Idaho, Montana, and Wyoming. The park started in 1872. It was the first national park. The park has geysers. Geysers are springs. Water sprays out of the ground!

Many animals live in Yellowstone National Park. There are grizzly bears. There are wolves. There are groups of bison.

This photo was taken in 1931. There are groups of people. Some are on horses. They are looking at the canyon. They are also looking at the Lower Falls of the Yellowstone River. This part of the river is in Wyoming.

Library of Congress, LC-USZ62-126295

Yellowstone

Yellowstone is a national park. It is in three states. That is a very big park! It is in Idaho, Montana, and Wyoming. It started in 1872. It is the first national park. It has geysers. Geysers are springs. Water shoots out of the ground!

Many animals live in Yellowstone National Park. There are grizzly bears and wolves. There are even groups of bison.

This photo was taken in 1931. There are groups of people. Some are on horses. They are looking at the canyon. They are also looking at the Lower Falls of the Yellowstone River. This part of the river is in Wyoming.

Library of Congress, LC-USZ62-126295

Yellowstone

 Investigate

1. What do you see in this photo?

   _____

   _____

2. What did you see first? Why?

   _____

   _____

 Question

3. Look at the photo. What do you want to learn more about?

   _____

   _____

4. Did you ever see a spring or a geyser? What do you remember about it?

   _____

   _____

Understand

5. What do you think the Lower Falls in Yellowstone look like today? Look it up!

   _____

   _____

6. What clues tell you this picture was not taken yesterday?

   _____

   _____

Mount Rushmore

Mount Rushmore is in the Black Hills. The Black Hills are in South Dakota. Mount Rushmore is a mountain. Four faces are on it. The faces are men. The men were US presidents. George Washington and Thomas Jefferson are on the left. Theodore Roosevelt and Abraham Lincoln are on the right.

People like to see the mountain. It is made of rock. The rock is granite. It is good to carve. The sun hits the faces in the day. Lights shine on it at night.

The photo is from 1932. The artist is on a nose! It is George Washington's nose! The artist is Gutzon Borglum. The inspector is on the nose with him! Do you know how long it took the artist to carve the rock? It took 14 years!

Library of Congress, LC-USZ62-63648

Mount Rushmore

Mount Rushmore is in the Black Hills. It is in South Dakota. Mount Rushmore is a mountain. It has faces on it. The faces belong to four men. The men were US presidents. They are George Washington and Thomas Jefferson. They are Theodore Roosevelt and Abraham Lincoln.

Every year, visitors go see Mount Rushmore. It is made of a rock. The rock is called granite. It is good to carve. This side of the mountain gets lots of sun in the day. At night, lights shine on it.

The photo is from 1932. The artist is standing on a nose! It is George Washington's nose! The artist's name is Gutzon Borglum. An inspector is on the nose with him! Do you know how long it took Gutzon to carve Mount Rushmore? It took 14 years!

Library of Congress, LC-USZ62-63648

Mount Rushmore

Mount Rushmore is in the Black Hills. It is in South Dakota. It is a mountain. It has faces carved into it. The faces belong to four men. The men were US presidents. They are George Washington and Thomas Jefferson. They are Theodore Roosevelt and Abraham Lincoln.

Every year, visitors go see the great mountain. It is made of a rock called granite. It is good to carve. This side of the mountain gets lots of sun in the day. At night, lights shine on it.

The photo was taken in 1932. The artist is perched on George Washington's nose! The artist's name is Gutzon Borglum. An inspector is also on George's nose! Do you know how long it took Gutzon to carve Mount Rushmore? It took 14 years!

Library of Congress, LC-USZ62-63648

Name _____

Mount Rushmore

 Investigate

1. What do you see in this photo?

   _____

   _____

2. What did you see first? Why?

   _____

   _____

 **Question**

3. Look at the photo. What do you want to learn more about?

   _____

   _____

4. Have you ever seen a mountain? When? Tell what you saw.

   _____

   _____

 Understand

5. Why are the men on the nose? How do they stay there?

   _____

   _____

6. Compare a picture of George Washington with this photo. What do you see? Does the rock face look like him?

   _____

   _____

Giant Sequoia

Sequoia National Park is in California. It has lots of giant trees. They are sequoias. They grow to be very tall. They are more than 300 feet (90 meters) tall! They are in a forest.

The trees are old. They are the oldest trees. Some are 2,000 years old! Many trees are in the park. There are more than 8,000!

The photo is from 1910. This car was the first one to drive in the park! The car looks different from cars today. It looks small next to the tree. The car is normal size. But, the tree is big! Look how wide the tree trunk is! The trunk is part of the tree. It is the bottom of the tree. Did you ever see a tree this big?

25 H.P. 'Hudson' owned by H.T. Mayo, Visalia Cal. First Auto to enter Sequoia National Park— July 14:'10

Giant Sequoia

Sequoia National Park has many giant trees. The sequoias grow there. They are very big! They are more than 300 feet (90 meters) tall! They are in California.

Sequoias are old. They are the oldest trees. Some are 2,000 years old! More than 8,000 sequoias are in the park.

The photo is from 1910. The car was the first one to enter the park! The car is from more than 100 years ago. It looks small. It is a normal size car. But, the tree is so big! Look at how wide the tree trunk is. The trunk is the bottom of the tree. Have you ever seen a tree so big?

25 H.P. 'Hudson' owned by H.T. Hays, Visalia Cal. First Auto to enter Sequoia National Park— July 14 '10

Giant Sequoia

Sequoia National Park is the home to many giant trees. Sequoias grow very large. They are more than 300 feet (90 meters) tall! They are in California.

Sequoias are the oldest trees. Some are 2,000 years old! More than 8,000 sequoias are in the forest in the park.

The photo was taken in 1910. This car was the first to enter the park! The car is from over 100 years ago. It seems very small. It is a normal size car. But, the tree is so big! Look at how wide the tree trunk is. The trunk is the bottom of the tree. Have you ever seen a tree so big?

25 H.P. 'Hudson' owned by H.T. Mayo, Visalia Cal. First Auto to enter Sequoia National Park— July 14 '10

Name _____

Giant Sequoia

 Investigate

1. What do you see in this photo?

   _____

   _____

2. What did you see first? Why?

   _____

   _____

 Question

3. Look at the photo. What do you want to learn more about?

   _____

   _____

4. Compare the tree and the car. Which is wider? How do you know?

   _____

   _____

 Understand

5. Why is the trunk so wide?

   _____

   _____

6. Why do you think the man visited the park?

   _____

   _____

Harriet Tubman

Harriet Tubman is a famous person. She led many slaves to freedom. She was a worker on the Underground Railroad. It was not a real railroad. It was a route that led people to freedom in the North.

Harriet helped during a war. It was the Civil War. She helped the Union side. The Union Army was in the North. She was also a spy. She was a cook. Harriet had many jobs. She was born a slave, but she was very strong. She wanted all slaves to be free.

The photo was taken between 1860 and 1875. Harriet wears a shirt with a fancy collar and lots of buttons. She wears a long skirt. Her hands are on the back of the chair. She looks proud.

Library of Congress, LC-USZ62-7816

Harriet Tubman

Harriet Tubman is a famous person. She is African American. She led many slaves to freedom. She was a worker on the Underground Railroad. It was not a real railroad. It was a route that led people to freedom in the North.

Harriet helped the Union Army. She helped during the Civil War. She was a spy. She was a cook. She was a nurse. Harriet had many jobs. She may have been born a slave, but she was very strong. She wanted all slaves to have freedom.

The photo was taken between 1860 and 1875. Harriet wears a shirt with a fancy collar and many buttons. She wears a long skirt. Her hands are on the back of the chair. She looks proud.

Library of Congress, LC-USZ62-7816

Harriet Tubman

Harriet Tubman is a famous person. She is African American. She led many people to freedom. The people were slaves. Harriet was a worker on the Underground Railroad. It was not a real railroad. It was a route that led people to freedom in the North.

Harriet helped the Union Army during the Civil War. She was a spy. She was a cook. She was a nurse. Harriet had many jobs. She may have been born a slave, but she was a very strong woman. She wanted all slaves to have freedom in America.

The photo was taken between 1860 and 1875. Harriet wears a shirt with a fancy collar and many buttons. She wears a long skirt. Her hands are on the back of the chair. She looks proud.

Library of Congress, LC-USZ62-7816

Harriet Tubman

 **Investigate**

1. What do you see in this photo?

   _____

   _____

2. What did you see first? Why?

   _____

   _____

 Question

3. Look at the photo. What do you want to learn more about?

   _____

   _____

4. What was the Underground Railroad? Why was it important?

   _____

   _____

Understand

5. What face is Harriet making? What do you think she was thinking about when her picture was taken?

   _____

   _____

6. Why do you think Harriet had so many jobs?

   _____

   _____

Laddie Boy

Laddie Boy was a dog. But, he was not just any dog. He was the president's dog! He lived at the White House. He was there from 1921 to 1923. Presidents live in the White House. It is in Washington, DC.

Laddie Boy was President Harding's dog. He was a terrier. He was a nice dog. He was loved. He even had his own chair!

The photo is from July 25, 1922. That day was great for Laddie Boy. It was his birthday! He is next to a big cake. Is the cake made with dog snacks? Is it made with real cake? He is a lucky dog!

Laddie Boy

Laddie Boy was a dog. But, he was not just any dog. He was the president's dog! He lived at the White House. It is where presidents live. The White House is in Washington, DC.

President Harding's dog was named Laddie Boy. He was a terrier. Laddie Boy lived in the White House from 1921 to 1923. He was loved. He had many friends. He had a special chair!

The photo is from July 25, 1922. It was Laddie Boy's birthday! A big cake is in the photo. Is the cake made with dog snacks? Is it made with real cake? He is a lucky dog!

Library of Congress, LC-USZ62-131899

Laddie Boy

Laddie Boy was a dog. But, he was not a regular dog. He was a president's dog! He lived at the White House. The White House is where presidents live. The White House is in Washington, DC.

Laddie Boy was President Harding's dog. Laddie Boy was a national dog. He was an Airedale terrier. He was a White House pet from 1921 to 1923. He was loved. He even had his own special chair!

The photo is from 1922. It was taken on July 25 because that was Laddie Boy's birthday! He had a big cake. The cake was sent to Laddie Boy from the people at the kennel where he was born. Is it made with dog treats? He is a lucky Laddie Boy!

Library of Congress, LC-USZ62-131899

Laddie Boy

 Investigate

1. What do you see in this photo?

   _____

   _____

2. What did you see first? Why?

   _____

   _____

   _____

 Question

3. Look at the photo. What do you want to learn more about?

   _____

   _____

4. Tell about a dog you have met. How was it different from Laddie Boy?

   _____

   _____

 Understand

5. Name another pet that lives or has lived at the White House.

   _____

   _____

6. What do you think Laddie Boy's party was like? Who was there? What did they do? What did they eat?

   _____

   _____

The President and Tad

Abraham Lincoln was a president of the United States. He was number 16. President Lincoln had four kids. His youngest boy was Tad.

Tad was the little one. Tad's name was Thomas. He had the same name as his grandpa. But, President Lincoln called him "Tad." Tad looked like a little tadpole when he was born! Abraham Lincoln thought Tad was small and cute.

The photo is from 1864. The president and Tad are close. They are sitting next to each other. They are looking at a photo album together. They are having a good time. They are father and son.

Library of Congress, LC-USZ62-11897

The President and Tad

Abraham Lincoln was a president of the United States. He was the 16th president. His youngest son was Tad.

President Lincoln had four kids. Tad was the little one. Tad's real name was Thomas. He had the same name as his grandpa. But, Abe Lincoln called him "Tad" because he looked like a little tadpole when he was born! His dad thought he was small and cute.

The photo is from 1864. The president and Tad are close. They are sitting next to each other. They are looking at a photo album together. They are having a good time. They are father and son.

Library of Congress, LC-USZ62-11897

The President and Tad

Abraham Lincoln was a president of the United States. He was the 16th president. He had a son named Tad.

Tad was Abraham Lincoln's youngest son. Tad's real name was Thomas. He was named after his grandfather. But, President Lincoln called him "Tad" because he looked like a little tadpole when he was born! His dad thought he was small and cute.

The photo is from 1864. The president is Tad's father. They are sitting next to each other. They are looking at a photo album together. They are having a good time. They are father and son.

Library of Congress, LC-USZ62-11897

The President and Tad

 **Investigate**

1. What do you see in this photo?

   _____

   _____

2. What did you see first? Why?

   _____

   _____

 Question

3. Look at the photo. What do you want to learn more about?

   _____

   _____

4. Why do you think this photo is famous?

   _____

   _____

Understand

5. What do you think Tad and his father are talking about while they look at the album?

   _____

   _____

6. Why do they seem to be dressed up?

   _____

   _____

The Statue of Liberty

The Statue of Liberty was a gift. France gave it to the United States. It showed friendship. It meant freedom.

Sometimes people left their countries. When they got to America, they saw this statue. They saw it from their boats. It was a symbol of freedom. It made people feel great. They were happy to come and start a new life.

The drawing is from 1877. People are in the boat. The boat is in the water. It is by New York City. The people are ready to come to the "land of the free." They see the statue. Let freedom ring!

© Carson-Dellosa • CD-104860 • Evidence-Based Inquiry Using Primary Sources

The Statue of Liberty

The Statue of Liberty was a present. France gave it to the United States. It showed friendship. It showed freedom.

Sometimes people left their countries. When they got to America, they saw this statue. It was a symbol of freedom. It made people feel free. They were happy to come to America and start a new life.

The drawing is from 1877. People are in the boat. The boat is in the water. It is near New York City. The people are ready to come to the "land of the free." The Statue of Liberty is in the background. Let freedom ring!

NEW YORK.—WELCOME TO THE LAND OF FREEDOM—AN OCEAN STEAMER PASSING THE STATUE OF LIBERTY: SCENE ON THE STEERAGE DECK.

The Statue of Liberty

The Statue of Liberty was a present. France gave it to the United States in 1886. It showed friendship. It showed freedom.

Sometimes people left their countries. When some people got to America, they saw this statue. It was a symbol of freedom. It made people feel free. They were happy to come to America and start a new life.

The drawing is from 1877. People are in the boat. The boat is in the water. It is near New York City. The people are ready to come to the "land of the free." The Statue of Liberty is in the background. Let freedom ring!

The Statue of Liberty

 Investigate

1. What do you see in this drawing?

    _____

    _____

2. What did you see first? Why?

    _____

    _____

 **Question**

3. Look at the photo. What do you want to learn more about?

    _____

    _____

4. Did you ever see this statue? If not, tell about a statue you have seen.

    _____

    _____

 Understand

5. Why are the people in the boat? What do you think they are thinking?

    _____

    _____

6. What would it feel like to move to another country?

    _____

    _____

Song of Freedom

"The Star-Spangled Banner" is a famous song. It is America's song. Francis Scott Key wrote it. He wrote it during a war. The war was called the War of 1812.

Many people in the army sang this song in the war. The song made them think of freedom. It was not America's song until 1931. President Hoover said it was time.

The print is from 1861. An artist drew it. The children are singing. They are singing "The Star-Spangled Banner." The lady plays the piano for the children. It must sound nice!

Library of Congress, LC-USZ62-5264

Song of Freedom

"The Star-Spangled Banner" is a well-known song. It is America's song. Francis Scott Key wrote it during a war. The war was called the War of 1812.

Many people in the army sang this song in the war. It was a song with words of freedom. It was not America's official song until 1931. President Hoover said it was time.

The print is from 1861. An artist drew it. The children sing a song. They are singing "The Star-Spangled Banner." The lady plays the piano for the children. It must sound nice!

Library of Congress, LC-USZ62-5264

Song of Freedom

"The Star-Spangled Banner" is a famous song. It is America's song. It was written by Francis Scott Key during a war. The war was called the War of 1812.

Many people in the army sang this song in the war. It was a song that made them think of freedom. It was not America's official song until 1931. President Hoover said it was time.

The print is from 1861. An artist drew it. The children are singing. They are singing "The Star-Spangled Banner." The lady plays the piano for the children. It must sound nice!

Library of Congress, LC-USZ62-5264

Song of Freedom

 Investigate

1. What do you see in this print?

   _____

   _____

2. What did you see first? Why?

   _____

   _____

? **Question**

3. Look at the photo. What do you want to learn more about?

   _____

   _____

4. Do you sing this song? Have you heard other people sing it? When?

   _____

   _____

 Understand

5. Why did the artist draw this print?

   _____

   _____

6. What room do you think they are singing in? How can you tell?

   _____

   _____

Friends with Flags

America's flag changed. In 1777, it had 13 white stars. It had 13 red and white stripes. Later, a star was added for each new state. Now the flag has 50 stars.

The colors have meaning. The white is for being pure. The red is for being brave. The blue is for being fair. The stars are a symbol of the heavens or space.

The photo was taken between 1910 and 1915. There are six boys. They are on a playground. The playground is in New York. The boys hold American flags in their hands.

Library of Congress, LC-DIG-ggbain-14003

Friends with Flags

America's flag changed. In 1777, it had 13 white stars. It had 13 red and white stripes. Later, a star was added for each new state. And, now the flag has 50 stars.

The colors have meaning. The white is for pureness. The red is for bravery. The blue is for fairness. The stars are a symbol of the heavens or space.

The photo was taken between 1910 and 1915. The boys are on a playground. They are in New York. The boys hold American flags in their hands.

Library of Congress, LC-DIG-ggbain-14003

Friends with Flags

America's flag changed. In 1777, it had 13 white stars. It had 13 red and white stripes. Later, a star was added for each new state. And, now the flag has 50 stars.

The colors each mean something. The white is for pureness. The red is for bravery. The blue is for fairness. The stars are a symbol of the heavens or space.

The photo is from between 1910 and 1915. The boys are on a playground. They are in New York. The boys have American flags in their hands.

Friends with Flags

 Investigate

1. What do you see in this photo?

    _____

    _____

2. What did you see first? Why?

    _____

    _____

 Question

3. Look at the photo. What do you want to learn more about?

    _____

    _____

4. Is there a flag at your school? Where? What do you think about when you see it?

    _____

    _____

 Understand

5. Why do you think the boys have flags out on the playground?

    _____

    _____

6. What does the flag mean to you?

    _____

    _____

Answer Key

Page 7

1. librarian; children studying, working, and reading, tables, books; 2. Answers will vary. 3. Answers will vary. 4. Answers will vary. 5. Answers will vary. 6. Answers will vary but should relate to common library practices.

Page 11

1. traffic policeman, girls, horse-drawn wagon; 2. Answers will vary. 3. Answers will vary. 4. They help people stay safe on the roads. 5. He wants the girls to cross the street safely. He wants the car to stop. 6. Answers will vary.

Page 15

1. dog, teacher, students, chalkboard; 2. Answers will vary. 3. Answers will vary. 4. It is being used for teaching a lesson. 5. They could be learning about the dog, about living things, or about how to take care of pets. 6. Answers will vary.

Page 19

1. shells, children, adults, baby; 2. Answers will vary. 3. Answers will vary. 4. Kids worked many years ago to help their families. 5. work clothes, pants and shirts, dresses; 6. children, adults, baby

Page 23

1. horse, words, chickens, sheep, pigs, cows; 2. Answers will vary. 3. Answers will vary. 4. Answers will vary. 5. Gordon is the horse's name. 6. Poultry is chicken. Encourage students to list unfamiliar words and look them up.

Page 27

1. three boys, boxes of gum; 2. Answers will vary. 3. Answers will vary. 4. Answers will vary, but lead students to discover that 50 cents could buy a shirt or two quarts of milk then. 5. pants, work outfits, ties, shirts, hats. Answers will vary. 6. Answers will vary.

Page 31

1. Yellowstone, trees, car, river, people, waterfall; 2. Answers will vary. 3. Answers will vary. 4. Answers will vary. 5. They look almost exactly the same today. 6. car, clothing, camera

Page 35

1. George Washington, nose, two men; 2. Answers will vary. 3. Answers will vary. 4. Answers will vary.

5. They are inspecting the work done on the nose. The men use ropes or pulleys. 6. Answers will vary.

Page 39

1. sequoia trees, car, man; 2. Answers will vary. 3. Answers will vary. 4. The tree is wider. 5. The tree gets bigger as it gets older. 6. Answers will vary.

Page 43

1. Harriet Tubman, chair, hat; 2. Answers will vary. 3. Answers will vary. 4. It was a route to freedom for slaves. 5. She looks serious. Answers will vary. 6. Answers will vary but could include she always wanted to help people and do what was right.

Page 47

1. Laddie Boy, dog, cake; 2. Answers will vary. 3. Answers will vary. 4. Answers will vary. 5. Answers will vary but should focus on a White House pet in their lifetime. 6. Answers will vary but research would show that Laddie Boy's favorite people and dogs were invited. Other dogs shared the "cake."

Page 51

1. father and son, President Abraham Lincoln and Tad; 2. Answers will vary. 3. Answers will vary. 4. President Lincoln was a well-known president, and people cared for his son Tad. 5. Answers will vary but they may be discussing memories. 6. Answers will vary but could include that they were posing for a picture or that they were in the White House.

Page 55

1. boats, water, Statue of Liberty, people; 2. Answers will vary. 3. Answers will vary. 4. Answers will vary. 5. They are coming to America. Answers will vary. 6. Answers will vary.

Page 59

1. children, piano, lady; 2. Answers will vary. 3. Answers will vary. 4. Answers will vary. 5. Answers will vary but could include that the artist was trying to show a patriotic family or honor "The Star-Spangled Banner." 6. Answers will vary.

Page 63

1. boys, flags; 2. Answers will vary. 3. Answers will vary. 4. Answers will vary. 5. Answers will vary but may include they are marching in a line. 6. Answers will vary.